MATT HARTLEY

Matt studied Drama at the University of Hull. *Sixty Five Miles* won the Under-26 Prize in the inaugural Bruntwood Prize for Playwriting. In 2006–07 Matt was a member of Channel 4/Paines Plough Future Perfect Scheme. Other work for theatre includes: *The Bee* (Edinburgh Festival), *Punch* (Hampstead Theatre/Heat and Light Company), *Sentenced* (Union Theatre), *Epic* (Theatre503/Latitude) and *Trolls* for East 15 Drama School (Tristan Bates/Theatre503). Radio includes: *The Pursuit* for Radio 4. Television includes: *Hollyoaks* for Lime Pictures. Matt is currently under commission to the Royal Shakespeare Company and Lime Pictures.

Other Titles in this Series

Matt Hartley

SIXTY FIVE MILES

NICK HERN BOOKS

London

www.nickhernbooks.co.uk

A Nick Hern Book

Sixty Five Miles first published in Great Britain as a paperback original in 2012 by Nick Hern Books Limited, 14 Larden Road, London W3 7ST, in association with Paines Plough and Hull Truck Theatre

Cover photograph by Graham Michael
Cover design by Ned Hoste, 2H

Typeset by Nick Hern Books, London
Printed in the UK by Mimeo Ltd, Huntingdon, Cambridgeshire PE29 6XX

A CIP catalogue record for this book is available from the British Library

ISBN 978 1 84842 256 8

Sixty Five Miles was first produced by Hull Truck Theatre and Paines Plough, and performed at Hull Truck Theatre, Hull, on 1 February 2012, with the following cast:

PETE GILES	Craige Els
RICHARD GILES	Alan Morrissey
LINDA / MAGGIE ASHTON	Becci Gemmell
LUCY ASHTON / MICHELLE	Katie West
FRANK BURTON /	Ian Bleasdale
TONY ETHERINGTON	

Director	George Perrin
Designer	Amy Cook
Lighting Designer	Tim Deiling
Sound Designer/Composer	Edward Lewis

Acknowledgements

I am indebted to the following people for their support, love, loans, friendship and unwitting inspiration:

Mum, Dad, Dave, where to begin…

Nick Bagnall, Bear Loves Squid. George Perrin. My 'reet' good cast: Craige, Alan, Becci, Katie and Ian. James, Tara, Andrew and all at Paines Plough/Hull Truck for making this happen. The Peggy Ramsay Foundation and Bruntwood, for proving that supporting the arts is essential.

Dippy, Si, Matt B, Darren, Ad's, Booner, Tommy Robinson, Felix, Joey D, Brendan, Kate Mack, James Graham, Nicky Bunch, Sian Reese Williams, Nick Tennant, Jo Leather, Rick Laxton, Joel Horwood, DC Moore, Al Smith, Adam Brace, Simon Stephens, Amy Thompson, Hattie Crisell, Chris Brandon, Tim Roseman, Paul Robinson, Claire Birch, Will Mortimer, Tobes, Lisa Spirling, Pippa Hill, Sam Rotherham, Ben H-B, Mikey, Amy Michaels, Jess and Cameron Christie, Nick Quinn and all at the Agency.

Matt Hartley

For my brother (Blades)

Characters

PETE GILES, *early thirties*
RICHARD GILES, *early twenties*
LUCY SPENCER, *early twenties*
LINDA, *late forties*
FRANK BURTON, *late fifties*
MAGGIE SPENCER, *late forties*
MICHELLE, *fifteen years old*
TONY ETHERINGTON, *early forties*

Location

Sheffield and Hull.

Time

November, 2005.

A forward slash (/) within a line indicates the next speaker interrupts.

A forward slash (/) at the end of a line indicates continued speech.

This text went to press before the end of rehearsals and so may differ slightly from the play as performed.

ONE

Eleven a.m.

RICH*'s living room.*

PETE *stands facing* RICH, *a very small suitcase by his feet.*

Silence.

PETE. 'An't changed, 'as it?

RICH. No.

PETE. Still the same tatty wallpaper.

RICH. Yeah.

PETE. This fucking carpet.

 PETE *stares round the room.*

RICH. A put a shelf up.

PETE. Yeah?

RICH. But it fell down. Was there.

PETE. Right.

RICH. 'Ardly anything on it. Just a couple of books.

PETE. Is that right?

RICH. No real pressure on the shelf. Just gave way. Think I must just be crap at DIY. So haven't bothered t'put it back up again.

PETE. Probably right. Don't want loads of fucking... / marks.

RICH. / Holes.

PETE. On the walls. Exactly, yeah.

RICH. Yeah.

 Silence.

PETE. Dirty though. Could do with a fucking clean, yer know. All this dust.

RICH. A do clean.

PETE. Make yerself ill if you don't.

Pause.

Feels strange. /

RICH. So it should.

PETE. / Back in this house.

Pause.

This fucking carpet.

RICH. Small bag.

PETE. What?

RICH. Just sayin', that's a small bag.

PETE. Are yer tekin the piss?

RICH. No, just… It's a small bag that's all.

PETE. Are you trying to make this more awkward than it already is?

RICH. No.

PETE. Because I don't need that.

Pause.

RICH. Just I never seen one that small before.

PETE. What?

RICH. That. I just never seen somert so tiny. Not for clothes.

PETE. Don't'ave much stuff that's why.

RICH. Right. Right. Not much stuff, right.

PETE. That's why I've got it. This little thing. Fuckin'. Camp little, what would you call it, suitcase? /

RICH. Handbag.

PETE. / Couple shirts. Pair of trousers. Photo or two. Letters. That's all. Yer know? Look. Look at this. It has this. Has a handle. Pull it up. Helps yer t'drag it. Saves yer from carryin' it. Imagine doing that…

RICH. D'yer want me t'take it f'yer?

PETE *waves the question away.*

PETE. Feel like a should tek me shoes off.

RICH. Can do.

PETE. But I'm not going to. No point is the'. This fuckin' carpet. Like tar. Like walkin' on tar. Should just rip it up.

RICH. Is that right.

PETE. My opinion anyway. Never liked it. Look at that mark. Dirty big stain –

RICH. It's just a mark, right. Not the end of the world.

PETE. No. No, I suppose not.

Very long silence.

So.

RICH. So?

Beat.

What?

PETE. Yer know?

RICH. What?

PETE. Yer read me letter.

RICH. Only one yer sent me.

PETE. Don't be precious.

RICH. Just sayin'.

PETE. Yer read it.

RICH. Yes.

PETE. And?

RICH. Pete. Don't think it were fair.

PETE. Rich.

RICH. What you asked of me. Don't you think?

PETE. Rich.

RICH. I don't think it were fair.

PETE. Rich, don't make me spell it out.

RICH. No.

PETE. No?

RICH. No. Didn't leave an address. Nothing.

PETE. Okay, okay, okay.

Pause.

Okay.

RICH. Wish you 'adn't asked me t'do it.

PETE. Yer tried Emma's family?

RICH. Felt awkward. Well fuckin' awkward.

PETE. Yer tried Emma's mum?

RICH. Why you suddenly interested? Never bothered before.

PETE. Yer try Emma's mum?

RICH. No.

PETE. She still live up –

RICH. I don't even know who she is, Pete.

PETE. No, no, no.

Beat.

No?

RICH. No.

PETE. No, I guess yer wouldn't.

Pause.

RICH. D'yer want some cake?

PETE. Cake?

RICH. Yeah.

PETE. Is that what the smell is?

RICH. Just tried out a recipe.

PETE. Nah, I'll be alright.

Silence.

PETE *lifts the handle on the suitcase up then pushes it back down.*

Silence.

Can I have a cup of tea though? I'd like a cup of tea.

RICH. Yer staying then?

PETE. Yeah.

RICH. Not just going to piss off.

PETE. No. Need t–

RICH. Cos your old room, that's mine now.

PETE. Right.

RICH. Has been for ages. You'll have to sleep in my old room. Bunk beds. You'll be alright with that won't you? Used t'them.

Silence.

Suppose I could get you some fresh sheets. Put them in Mum's. You'll have t'clear the stuff off it though.

PETE. Nine years.

RICH. Nine 'n'alf.

PETE. Thought yer might have grown a little.

RICH. Fuck off.

PETE. Least a couple of inches.

RICH. Grown a lot. Learned a lot.

PETE. Bit of a short-arse really.

RICH. Sorry?

PETE. Yer quite short, aren't yer?

RICH. Not short. Average mebee but not short.

PETE. 'Ow tall are yer then?

RICH. I dunno.

PETE. 'Bout five nine.

RICH. I dunno.

PETE. Mebee five eight.

RICH. I don't fuckin' know, yeah!

Pause.

Pete, yer should know. This is my house right. Yer just a guest.

Silence. PETE *takes a photo off the top of the television. Stares at it. Looks at* RICH. *Looks at the photo.*

PETE. Certainly take after me mum. Same haircut. /

RICH. Fuck off.

PETE. / S'uncanny.

RICH. Fuck off.

PETE. Apart from the language on yer.

RICH. Put that back.

RICH *puts his hand down the front of his trousers.*

Put it back, Pete.

PETE *does.*

PETE. Yer still stick yer hand down yer trousers when yer nervous.

RICH. I'm not nervous.

PETE. I'd rather yer were nervous than aroused.

RICH. You've got some fucking nerve.

PETE *stares at* RICH. RICH *wavers.*

Meant t'be at work yer know.

PETE. No.

Beat.

RICH. Well, I am. But I took the day off. Not getting holiday pay or nothing. Just took it off. Hope yer happy that I'm going t'be poorer.

PETE. I'm going t'need t'borrow yer car over the next month or so.

Pause.

RICH. Mum dunt know yer stayin' 'ere yer know?

PETE. No?

RICH. Talkin' about you still upsets her.

PETE. –

RICH. She's proud of me.

PETE. Yeah.

RICH. Thought yer should know that.

Pause.

PETE. Do you want a badge, is that what yer want?

RICH. Shut up.

PETE. Little fucking badge. Pin it t'yer shirt.

RICH. No.

PETE. Mummy's boy, written on it.

RICH. No.

PETE. Then what you fucking saying that for?

RICH goes to puts his hands down his trousers, stops himself.

RICH. Not funny, yer know. Not laughin'.

Pause.

Nine years and I didn't even get a fuckin' hello.

PETE. Nine years, six months, eleven days.

Pause. RICH exits. PETE rubs his eyes. Stares round the room. RICH returns.

What?

RICH. How do yer 'ave yer tea?

PETE. Me?

RICH. A don't have to ask meself do I. Kinda know that myself. Course you.

PETE. Yer don't remember.

RICH. Just asked yer didn't I? Surely that answers yer question.

PETE. You used to always make me my tea. On a Saturday. *Football Focus*. I'd come round. Hungover. Yer'd bring me a cup of tea.

RICH. Right.

PETE. Yer used t'do that.

RICH. I believe yer. 'N' how did yer use t'ave yer tea?

PETE. Just milk.

RICH. Right.

> RICH *goes to exit.*

PETE. But –

RICH. What?

PETE. Well, that was then.

RICH. Then?

PETE. Now a have it different.

RICH. Christ –

PETE. Just that sugar's one of the only luxuries yer can get hold of easily.

> *Pause.*

Two sugars.

> RICH *exits into the kitchen.* PETE *remains standing. Looks round. Retches. Bends his knees, puts his hand over his mouth.* RICH *enters, watches* PETE *in this position. Eventually…*

Fucking… strange, yeah…

RICH. Right.

> *Long pause.*

PETE. I got the train down.

RICH. Okay.

PETE. And when I got off at the station. Thought I'd got off at wrong place.

RICH. Town's changed.

PETE. Too right. Everything's shiny.

RICH. Just be grey in a few years.

PETE. And I just stood there. Staring. Not knowing what to do. Then I thought, I'm going to just smash this place up, tear it apart –

RICH. You didn't?

PETE *shakes his head.*

PETE. Just walked here instead.

RICH. Shouldn't say things like that. Especially after what you did. People believe that you'd actually do it.

PETE. –

RICH. Sit down, will yer.

PETE. What did yer say?

RICH. Why don't you sit down?

RICH *hands him a cup of tea. He has a piece of cake on a plate as well.* PETE *drinks.*

PETE. Nice.

RICH. 'Ardly rocket science, is it.

PETE. 'Arder than it looks.

RICH. It's not really, is it?

PETE. No.

RICH. Then why d'yer say it?

Pause.

PETE. Is that the cake?

RICH. One yer didn't want any of.

RICH *starts to eat the cake.*

PETE. They lettin' yer make the desserts now?

RICH. –

PETE. I'll be yer guinea pig.

RICH. –

PETE. Best try it on me. Before yer poison yer customers.

RICH. Yer do read my letters then.

PETE. Never read anythin' about yer poisonin' yer customers.

RICH. Fuck off.

PETE. I know yer a chef if that's what yer getting at.

RICH. Coulda replied t'one of them.

Silence.

Yer know yer shoulda fuckin' done. Twice. After all this time, s'not enough. Yer might as well be a stranger.

Silence. PETE *stands up and moves around the room. Stops. Cups his hands and rubs his face. Lets his hands fall to his side.*

PETE. I wanted it t'be rainin' when I got out. Wanted t'feel it. Love rain. On my skin. Freshness of it.

RICH. Not talkin' about the weather are yer? Only boring tossers speak about the weather.

PETE. I'm talking about me. Couldn't put the feelings in words. Couldn't write them down.

RICH. Coulda phoned.

PETE. Couldn't say them either.

RICH. Well, yer a bit screwed then.

PETE. I'm trying now.

Silence.

She were fifteen last week.

RICH. She probably won't even want t'see you.

PETE. Because of me there is a fifteen-year-old girl in this world. Amazes me.

RICH. Yer weren't even there when she were born.

Silence.

PETE. Life's about mistakes. Making them. Then learning.

RICH. No. That's not good enough.

PETE. We've all done things we regret. Don't go thinking you're a fucking angel.

RICH. Compared to you I'm Jesus.

PETE. I've just done things on a bigger scale.

RICH. Colossal, that's what scale.

PETE. Shut up.

RICH. You shut up.

PETE. No, you shut –

RICH. I told people that you were dead.

Beat.

PETE. What?

RICH. Wasn't going t'tell you. But I told people that you were dead. That's what I told them when they asked about my family.

PETE *starts to laugh.*

'S not funny. Truth. I did.

PETE *slowly stops to laugh.*

PETE. See you've done somert that you regret.

RICH. That doesn't keep me up at night.

PETE. No?

RICH. No.

Pause.

PETE. But somert does. Dunt it?

Pause. RICH *puts his hands down his trousers. Removes it almost instantly.*

RICH. A think yer should go 'n'and 'ave a lie-down.

PETE. 'Ave a shower.

RICH. Freshen up.

Long pause.

PETE. You stayin' in?

RICH. Not fuckin' workin', am I?

PETE *starts to exit, carrying his suitcase. Stops. Turns back round.*

PETE. Rich.

RICH. Yeah?

Silence.

That bag is the biggest fuckin' joke. Look a right prick.

Pause. PETE *exits.* RICH *stands. Fade.*

TWO

A few days later. A small shop that specialises in chocolates, Chesterfield. There is nobody behind the counter. RICH *enters. A door pings.*

LUCY (*off*). I'll be with yer in a minute.

RICH *goes to respond, doesn't. He looks around the shop. Takes a deep breath. Puts his hand down his trousers. Removes his hand. Looks round again. Rubs his face.* LUCY *enters, drying her hands with a towel. She goes to speak but stops as soon as she sees* RICH.

RICH. Look at you.

LUCY. Rich.

RICH. Look at you.

Silence. She puts the towel down.

Look at you.

LUCY. Yeah.

RICH. I like the hat.

LUCY. Have to wear them.

RICH. For health and safety.

LUCY. For health and safety.

RICH. Not fashion.

LUCY. No.

RICH. Hardly a fashion statement is it?

LUCY. No.

RICH. Not a fashion parade.

LUCY. Just stops my hair getting in the food.

RICH. I have to wear one as well. At work.

LUCY. This is out of the blue.

RICH. Yeah.

Pause.

Yeah it is, I suppose.

LUCY. You shoulda let me know.

RICH. Yeah.

LUCY. Can't just turn up like this.

RICH. Luce –

LUCY. It's not fair.

She picks up the towel. Dries an imaginary spot of water. Puts it down again. Silence. They stare at each other. Both break eye contact at the same time.

Have to finish wrapping these.

RICH. Sure. Sure.

LUCY. They're t'be collected. I 'ave t'do it.

RICH. Sure.

Silence. She starts to wrap the chocolates.

Got wet coming over.

Pause.

Walked from the train station.

Pause.

Not far is it? Ten minute walk or so.

LUCY. –

RICH. Rainin' that's why I got wet.

LUCY. Never.

RICH. Thought it were going t'tip it down. Thought I were going t'get drenched. Big dark cloud overhead.

LUCY. Don't start talking t'me about the weather.

RICH. It's conversation.

LUCY. I hate talking about the fucking weather. Can see it's raining, can't I? Christ. Just because yer good at letting people down dunt make yer a weather reporter!… Talking about the weather…

Long pause.

RICH. D'yer mind if I…?

LUCY. What?

RICH. Watch yer. Watch yer wrap them.

LUCY. Please, stop looking at me.

RICH. Look at you.

LUCY. Don't.

RICH. No. Please. Hear me out.

Pause. LUCY *stops wrapping, looks at* RICH. *Pause.*

Yer look well.

Pause.

LUCY. Is that it?

RICH. Just what a think. Looking at yer.

Long pause. LUCY *looks down at the floor. Then busies herself in the wrapping.*

Luce…

LUCY. –

RICH. Yer not gone deaf on me, 'ave yer?

LUCY *looks up. Pause. She goes back to wrapping the chocolates.*

They look nice.

LUCY. –

RICH. D' yer get t'eat them? Is that one a the perks?

LUCY. What?

RICH. The chocolates. Cakes.

LUCY. Are yer sayin' I've put weight on?

RICH. Did I say that?

LUCY. Sounds like yer sayin' I'm fat.

RICH. Yer not fat.

LUCY. I know I have. I know that I've put it on. Know that I'm bigger.

RICH. Yer still an okay size, yeah.

LUCY. But for you to swan in. No call. No nothing. And say that.

RICH. Look, forget I even mentioned it.

LUCY. It's not... fair. Don't yer think?

RICH *puts his face in his hands. Lets go. Looks at* LUCY. *Silence.*

RICH. My mum asked after yer.

LUCY. Rich.

RICH. She did. She liked you.

LUCY. Course she did. I'm lovely.

RICH. She's moved, yer know?

LUCY. No, I don't know. Why would I know? Why do people always say that? Yer know, when there's no way I would. 'S stupid.

RICH. Well, she's moved.

LUCY. Why are yer telling me this?

RICH. Moved in with Keith. Moved to Weymouth. It's –

LUCY. I know where Weymouth is.

RICH. Well, they got a cottage. Meant t'be nice. Ain't seen it. But it's meant t'be nice.

LUCY. What's this got t'do with me?

Pause.

RICH. I'll tell her yer said hi. That yer well.

LUCY. You'll tell her that I'm well?

RICH. Well, you are.

Beat.

Aren't yer?

Pause.

LUCY. My mum ain't asked after yer.

RICH. No surprise there.

LUCY. Not even one little query.

RICH. That because she's a stupid bitch. Sorry. No actually –

LUCY. Shut up, Rich.

Pause.

RICH. Nice shop this.

Pause.

LUCY. I like it.

RICH. Good smell.

LUCY. Course it's good. It's chocolate.

RICH. Nah. It's vanilla. Smells of vanilla pods. Reminds me of summer. Eating ice cream. Sitting outside in the sun. Lovely breeze about –

LUCY. Don't start talking about the fucking weather again!

Pause.

RICH. Get busy?

LUCY. Not right now.

RICH. No.

Pause.

LUCY. Can do. Can get really busy.

RICH. Yeah?

LUCY. Yeah.

Pause.

One time, they were queuing all the way round there.

RICH. Yeah?

LUCY. Never sell out though. Bob. Mr Watson. He's the owner. Always make sure it's stocked up well. Good like that.

RICH. Didn't think there'd be much call for a shop like this here.

LUCY. What's that mean?

RICH. Here. Chesterfield. Posh shop int it. Bet they're quite pricy them chocolates. Specialist. No Chezzy boys could afford these…?

LUCY. Shouldn't put this place down. Shouldn't sell people short like that.

RICH. Come on, it's Chezzy. Chez Vegas. Bloody dump. Any town that's major attraction is a church spire they fucked up, ain't got much going f'it.

LUCY. I like it.

RICH. Is that right?

LUCY. Yes, it is right. Got loads going f'it.

RICH. Like what?

LUCY. I'm not writing you a list. Don't 'ave t'sell it t'you. Obviously somert brought you here. Yeah?

Long pause.

I like the people.

RICH. Yer made some mates then?

LUCY. Mates?

RICH. Yer know, people that yer see. Go out with.

LUCY. Course. Course I have. A good bunch.

RICH. That's –

LUCY. Gemma. Gemma she works in the shop across the road. We go out have a laugh.

RICH. That's...

LUCY. She's nuts.

RICH. Have a good night out, yeah?

LUCY. Yeah.

RICH. Out on the town?

LUCY. Often, yeah.

RICH. Out in the bars?

LUCY. Got our regulars.

RICH. Givin' it large?

LUCY. With Gemma that's the only way. Non-stop. Larger than life.

RICH. Fat, yeah?

LUCY. No.

Pause.

She always attracts the lads.

RICH. All the dickheads, right?

LUCY. No. Some. Majority. The odd nice one though.

RICH. Yeah?

LUCY. Yeah.

Long pause.

Yeah.

RICH. Suppose yer close though aren't yer?

LUCY. Close?

RICH. To home. Only ten miles. Fifteen minutes on the train. That close, yer know, yer could come back easily. Just, yer know, visit. Or move back. Permanently. Is that somert you'd consider? D'yer think that's somert you would do?

Silence.

Not today. Or the day after. But, yer know, in the future.

Silence. LUCY looks away. Looks at the chocolates. Pushes them about. Not really achieving anything.

LUCY. I want t'tell yer somert.

RICH. Okay.

LUCY. It sounds daft.

RICH. I don't mind.

LUCY. No.

RICH. Go on.

LUCY. No. I…

RICH. Please.

LUCY looks out of the window. Rubs her hand on the towel. Looks back at RICH.

LUCY. D'yer know why I like workin' 'ere? And it's not being able to eat chocolate. It's the guessing. Imagining, yer know.

RICH. Imagining, right.

LUCY. Imagine all the stories behind why the chocolates are bought here. Yer know? Celebrations. Apologies. Hundreds of little stories. D'yer not think that's fascinating?

RICH. Yeah…

LUCY. And I think all these little stories up when I sell every little chocolate.

RICH. That's nice.

LUCY. It made me think. Yer know, yer remember the last time you bought me some chocolates. You remember that? You must do. Because it was the day before I went into hospital on my own.

RICH. Luce –

LUCY. And I thought, maybe, yer know. Maybe the person who you bought those chocolates from imagined a beautiful reason why you were buying them.

RICH. I –

LUCY. I really like that thought. Because it was such a bad choice.

Really bad thing to buy me.

Considering.

Perhaps you were buying them for our anniversary, yer know. That's what I hope they thought.

Not because.

Not be–

Not for.

RICH....L...

LUCY. Not before I –

Or because I'd just passed my driving test. That would...

Not...

Not so you felt.

So you could.

Avoid.

LUCY *stares at* RICH, *not sure what she is looking for.* RICH *cannot find any words.*

Suddenly the shop door opens. LINDA *enters. She is soaking wet. Shakes the water off her coat as she talks.*

LINDA. Hiya.

LUCY. Alright.

LINDA. Wet.

LUCY. Yes.

LINDA. Wet out there.

LUCY. Right.

LINDA. Really wet, wet, wet.

LUCY. Yes.

LINDA. Does nothing for my spirits, rain. Drizzle I can cope with. But rain. Rain makes me very, well, it lowers my libido considerably. Chocolates help to rouse me. Perk – (*To* RICH.) Sorry, were you waiting? I thought –

LUCY. What would you like?

LINDA. I'm not jumping the queue am I?

RICH *goes to speak, doesn't.*

Wouldn't want you to think I was –

LUCY. He's not in the queue.

LINDA. Oh. Right. Right. Lovely. Well then. Well. God, so many decisions. Aren't there so many choices? Could stay here all day –

LUCY. How about a selection?

LINDA. Well –

LUCY. That way you won't have t'decide. Shall we say one hundred grams?

LINDA. I tell you what I'd like.

LUCY. Yes?

LINDA. I'd like to try one. Could I try one?

LUCY. Try?

LINDA. Just to see if it's to my taste. The white rum truffle. I want to make sure I get the right ones.

Pause. LUCY *gives her a chocolate. She eats it, savouring every moment.*

Eventually –

Lovely. Lovely. That was lovely.

LUCY. Ten? Ten of these okay?

LINDA. Delicious. Absolutely delicious. But I think. I think it was the dark rum truffle I preferred.

Pause.

LUCY. You want to try one of those as well?

LINDA. If you wouldn't mind.

LUCY looks at LINDA, *takes a chocolate and passes it to* LINDA.

How kind.

LINDA *eats. She takes her time.*

Ah yes. Yes, that's the one.

LUCY. Shall I do ten then? Ten it is.

LUCY starts to count out ten chocolates and puts them in a bag. She puts the bag on the counter.

What?

LINDA. I'm sorry.

LUCY. You're not going t'buy these are yer?

LINDA. I have no money.

Pause.

Not a penny.

LUCY. Here. Take them. Take them.

LUCY passes LINDA *the chocolates.*

LINDA. Thank you. Thank you. Little angel you.

Silence.

Guess I'm back out to the, the, wet.

LUCY. Yes.

LINDA *lingers a second longer, then exits.*

What are you doing here?

RICH. I thought chocolates were a good idea.

LUCY. Chocolates don't make everything better, Rich.

RICH. Would flowers… or a card… been…?

LUCY. Why are yer here, Rich?

RICH. Are you going to have t'pay for…?

LUCY. What?

RICH. The truffles you gave that –

LUCY. Why are you here?

RICH. Here. Take this. I don't want you t'be out of pocket.

LUCY. Rich.

RICH. For me. Please.

LUCY. Don't you dare put that money on the counter.

Pause. He doesn't. Pause.

RICH. I wanted to see you.

LUCY. Why?

RICH. Can't believe –

LUCY. How did you know I was here?

RICH. Can't believe this doubt.

LUCY. Believe it. How?

RICH. You told me. Yer wrote t'me.

LUCY. When?

RICH. I don't…

LUCY. How long ago?

RICH. Wasn't –

LUCY. Six months ago. I wrote to you six months ago. Not a word. I haven't heard a single thing from you in that time. Don't tell me you've come here to see me. Don't insult me.

Silence.

RICH. My brother got let out. Pete. I let him move in. 'E's livin' with me. Got me thinkin'. Yer never met him.

LUCY. I know what 'e did though.

RICH. 'E's not a serial killer. 'E was a drunk twat who killed someone. 'N' now 'e dunt even know how to use a mobile phone. 'S funny. I let him have my old one and he just stands there looking at it.

LUCY. Am I meant t'be sad?

RICH. No.

LUCY. You want me t'feel sorry f'im?

RICH. No, I don't.

LUCY. Then why are yer telling me this? I don't even know him.

RICH. 'E made me think.

LUCY. Six months and this is what I get: your brother.

RICH. Do you want me t'go?

LUCY. Don't you dare try and walk away now.

RICH. Then let me fucking explain!

Pause.

I didn't want to shout then. I didn't come here to shout. I
didn't mean to do that. That's not me. It's not.

LUCY. No?

RICH. No.

Silence.

'E's looking f'is daughter. He's got a girl. Fifteen years old.
Dunt even know what she's called. Never heard from her.

LUCY. And what, this made you think of me? /

RICH. No. No. No. No.

LUCY. / You don't have a child.

RICH. Luce –

LUCY. Remember?

RICH. Yes. Yes. Yes. Yes I remember. Yes. But –

LUCY. You've no idea do yer?

RICH. Luce –

LUCY. Really. Really. Really don't.

RICH. Look.

Let me.

Try.

Let me try.

We've all done bad things.

I have.

We have.

That's what it made me realise.

And I know that I never.

I should have called.

Six months is.

I should have called.

Yes, I should have.

If I could go back through time I would.

But I was.

I'd be different as well, yer know.

I would.

If I could go back.

To you what I did.

To you what I did were.

To you what I did were.

To you.

Not. Not, maybe right.

It were not how I should have behaved.

Regardless of my feelings. Should have been more...

Do I mean sympathetic? I don't fucking know. I think so.
But...

And you fucking loved me as well which made it harder for
you.

And you still do. I see it in your eyes.

I just never felt the same.

Was close. So close. But.

I couldn't.

Something stopped me.

And that just made it that much easier for me.

Because it would have been a lie to carry on.

Just because of what we'd shared.

And we would have just dwelled on it.

I couldn't do that.

Because sometimes what I think we did were wrong.

You must do as well.

And t' be reminded of that is.

If we were together. That's what you'd do to me.

So what I'm trying to say is.

Why I came here.

I want to say.

Say this.

It's hard for me this...

The hospital. I should have been... And after I should have as well. You're right.

But I wasn't.

This is hard.

I'm finding this...

I want to say.

Say.

Not this. I want to say this.

It's such a simple thing to say. Normally.

Just not now.

I mean...

I mean...

I mean...

You must know what I mean.

Silence.

LUCY. I'm going t'go into the back and when I come out I'd like you t'ave gone.

> LUCY *exits. Shuts the door behind her.* RICH *stands still. Several seconds pass.* RICH *rubs his face. Several seconds pass.* RICH *takes out his wallet. Withdraws a twenty-pound note. Puts it back. Takes out a ten-pound note. Puts it on the counter.* RICH *lingers for several more seconds. Looks round. Exits. Fade.*

THREE

Four days later.

Froggatt Edge, Derbyshire.

RICH *is sat next to* FRANK.

PETE *is sat nearby.*

FRANK. 'S good t'get out of this city. Get some fresh air in the lungs. You can always spot a local. Yer know how, Rich?

RICH. How?

FRANK. They look healthy. Even the ugly ones. They've got a glow about them.

RICH. Yer should move 'ere then!

FRANK. Heh!

RICH. Heh!

FRANK. Would if I could. Expensive.

RICH. I like the drive.

FRANK. 'S not a racetrack. These little roads.

RICH. Romans definitely didn't build them.

FRANK. As long as yer careful.

PETE. He is.

> *Pause.*

FRANK (*to* RICH). Good.

RICH. Wouldn't let me go above forty.

FRANK. Sensible speed. How are yer, Rich?

RICH. I. A don't know, Frank.

FRANK. That good?

RICH. Yeah...

FRANK. How's that pretty girl?

Pause.

Oh.

RICH. I'm still cooking.

FRANK. Yer still cooking.

RICH. I am, yeah. You'll have to come round. Or I could. Whichever you.

FRANK. That'd be nice.

RICH. How's your work going?

FRANK. Same old. Same old. Just counting the days down.

RICH. What you up t'now?

FRANK (*instantly*). One thousand one hundred and twenty-nine. That's my sentence.

RICH. It'll be worth it in the end.

FRANK. Yeah. Old age. Great.

Silence.

RICH. Thanks f'comin'.

PETE. Didn't think yer would.

FRANK. Told yer, if yer ever needed me, Rich.

RICH. A know.

FRANK. Just didn't expect. A mean I heard he was out.

PETE. How did yer know?

FRANK. People talk.

PETE. Not t'me.

Silence.

FRANK. A brought yer here.

RICH. A know. Couple of times. Liked it. We went walkin'. Tried our hand at climbin'.

FRANK. Yeah. Is he stayin' with you?

RICH. Yeah.

FRANK. You alright with that?

PETE. I am here.

FRANK. Are yer?

RICH. 'S only whilst he gets settled. Looks f–

FRANK. Does yer mum… know?

RICH. Not yet.

FRANK. She should know.

PETE. Did yer ever get married in the end?

FRANK. Is he really askin' me that?

PETE. Yes.

FRANK *looks at* PETE *for a long time.*

FRANK. You've aged.

PETE. Has been ten years.

FRANK. Could be twenty lookin' at yer. Not like this one. Hasn't he grown into a fine specimen?

RICH. Leave it out.

FRANK. Spitting image of yer mother.

PETE. Don't want t'marry him too, do yer?

Pause.

FRANK. You. Well, you never took after her, did yer.

PETE. No. No, I suppose I didn't.

Pause.

RICH. You alright, Frank?

FRANK. Yes. Tell me, Pete. In all that time you had t'yerself, did yer do any reading?

PETE. Few books, you could say.

FRANK. Okay, 'n' out of that extensive number of books yer read. Did yer ever come across anythin' that hinted at the idea of: nature, nurture?

PETE. Mighta done.

FRANK. Because I think that you prove somert about nurture, 'n' that is, that it's all a load of shite. Sorry, Rich.

RICH. I've heard swear words before.

FRANK. See here's you two, 'n' you've both been treated exactly the same. Okay, so maybe yer dad gave you a couple more slaps than... Rich. But that's on account of him being around you longer.

PETE. Don't.

PETE *stands*.

RICH. Pete. Please, Frank, don't...

FRANK. Sorry, Rich. But yer mum loved yer both the same. She loved you rotten. Too much maybe. Yet, yer so different. See look at you now, clenching yer fist. Yer were born t'be like that. It's yer nature.

PETE. That means it's not my fault then. If I'm born t'be like this.

FRANK. Prove me wrong. And no I've not got married. I once asked a woman t'marry me. But a think yer know what she said.

Silence.

Why did yer want t'see me?

RICH. It was my idea.

FRANK. Because it hurts me a little, yer know.

RICH. Does it?

FRANK. Probably more than a little.

RICH. Wasn't my intention.

FRANK. A know. But what was?

PETE. It's for my benefit.

FRANK. Your benefit?

PETE. Taster of my 'andiwork, eh, Rich?

RICH. Somert like that.

PETE. A made your life hell, didn't I. Drove yer away.

FRANK. Yer mum made her decision.

RICH. 'N' she regretted it, yer know. I did as well.

FRANK. Well, that's very kind of yer. But we can't change the past.

PETE. No.

FRANK. As much as we'd like too.

PETE. A want t'find my daughter.

Silence.

RICH. 'E does.

FRANK. Think it's a bit of a cheek using that word. Why?

PETE. Why?

FRANK. After all this time.

PETE. I made her.

FRANK. Yer left her.

PETE. Will yer help me?

FRANK. Will I help you?

PETE. Yes.

Silence.

Yer don't know, do yer, what it's like to have the feeling, t'know that somert yer created is out there.

FRANK. Sadly not.

PETE. Well, it's started t'eat me up inside.

FRANK. But a tell yer what it's like t'nurture somert. T'care f'it so much. Regardless. You want it to be your own child. Own son. 'N' f'that t'be taken away. It's…

RICH. Frank…

FRANK. If life was fair you wouldn't find her. She deserves better.

Pause.

A won't help yer, Pete.

Silence.

PETE. Yer deserve t'enjoy your retirement.

FRANK. A know.

PETE. Yer'll be able t'make all them model airplanes you always go on about. Holidays…

FRANK. A just wanted someone t'spend it with.

Silence. FRANK *can't look at* PETE.

I'm going t'head back now.

RICH. Okay.

FRANK. If you ever. Yer know where I am.

RICH. A will.

FRANK. A hope so.

FRANK *exits, perhaps patting* RICH *on his shoulder as he goes. But at no point does he look at* PETE. *Silence.*

PETE. We'll stay a bit longer.

RICH. Oh, we will, will we?

PETE. Don't see these views every day.

RICH. He could have been my dad. But you. You.

PETE. Yeah… yeah.

Silence. RICH *looks away from* PETE. PETE *looks away from* RICH *and stares out.*

Fade.

FOUR

One week later. Bottom of The Moor. Sheffield town centre.
PETE *is sat next to a phone box. He has one of his hands*
covered from view. RICH *enters. He stares at* PETE.

RICH. People fuckin' piss there.

PETE. Don't care.

RICH. Can yer not smell it? Worse than a retirement home.

Pause.

Get up.

PETE. No.

RICH. People are looking.

PETE. Don't care.

RICH. I do.

PETE. Why?

RICH. It's embarrassing.

PETE. You took yer time.

RICH. Don't give me any of that.

PETE. Called yer an hour ago.

RICH. How d'yer think I got here? Yer took my fucking car. I
    'ad t'get the bus.

PETE. Yer such a kid.

RICH. What?

PETE. Whiny little tone.

RICH. I'm not a kid. Don't call me a kid.

PETE. Sound like one.

RICH. Fuck off.

PETE. Little fuckin' kid.

RICH. This is so fucking embarrassing this. If anyone saw me
    down here. Only right scrubbers hang round The Moor.

PETE. Ain't changed.

RICH. Exactly.

PETE. Don't recognise anywhere else.

RICH. I'm going to be late for work.

PETE. Sit.

RICH. I'm not here to chat. I'm here t'get my car.

PETE. Don't even care how I am.

RICH. Oh, don't give me that.

PETE. I've been driving all round today. Everywhere I could think.

RICH. Can't keep doing this to me, Pete.

PETE. And all the roads are different. Fucking proper nightmare.

RICH. What?

PETE. Like driving in a maze. Can't turn left. Can't turn right. No entry. One way. Fuckin'…

RICH. It's easy. All signposted.

PETE. 'S all changed. Used t'be able t'drive round with my eyes closed. Know every street. Coulda been a taxi driver no problem.

RICH. You drive too slow t'be a taxi driver. Too slow and in control.

PETE. All it is now. All it is now / is a maze. /

RICH. I know a maze.

PETE. / Like being at Chatsworth. Like being in the maze at Chatsworth.

RICH. I get yer.

PETE. But bigger and with more apartment blocks, yer know.

RICH. Pete.

PETE. Just going round in circles.

RICH. I get what happens in mazes. /

PETE. Got lost.

RICH. / Banging on about it. Like there's a fucking echo. Mazes, mazes, mazes.

PETE. Nothing wrong with driving slowly.

RICH. What?

PETE. Nothing wrong with being in control.

RICH. Did I say the' were?

PETE. Ask me what I've done today.

RICH. Pete.

PETE. Ask me, Rich.

RICH. Alright then but only if I can ask you a question first.

PETE. No.

RICH. What did yer think about f'those nine-and-a-half years? Did yer think about us?

PETE. Don't.

RICH. Yer family, did yer?

PETE. Don't.

RICH. Did yer think about me?

PETE. Don't.

RICH. Did yer?

PETE. Don't.

RICH. Because yer don't seem t'be now.

PETE. Mean it.

RICH. Well a hope yer did.

PETE. Don't.

RICH. A really 'ope yer fucking did.

PETE. D–

RICH. 'N' a really 'ope yer thought about all the things yer did as well.

PETE. Shut up.

RICH. Because I did. 'N' a 'ope it kept yer up at night. There –

PETE. Don't you ever fucking speak to me like that again.

PETE has stood up. PETE's *hand is seen for the first time. It's covered in blood.*

RICH. What have yer done?

PETE. Don't look at me like that.

RICH. Pete.

PETE. Sit fucking down.

Silence. RICH *sits.* PETE *remains standing.*

RICH. Tell me you've not done somert stupid.

Pause.

Pete, answer me. Please.

PETE. When you walk do yer look down?

RICH. What?

PETE. Do yer look down when your walkin'. Cos it struck me
    earlier that I always used to look down when I walked.
    Didn't care about where I was. Now though. Now I walk like
    this. Head up. Dead high. Scanning. Want to see everything.
    Every detail. Every single piece of my surroundings.

RICH. T'be honest, Pete, I fucking drive everywhere. So, yer
    know.

PETE. Don't say things like that, Rich. Don't say things like
    that. That's –

RICH. Pete –

PETE. No listen t'me. Every second somert new happens. On
    way back. Saw a woman. Old dotty little thing. She were by
    a postbox. Letter clasped in her hand. Hands so white they
    matched the envelope. And just before she posted it – Just at
    the second before it drops in with all the other fucking
    letters. She held back. Just for a second. But she hesitated.
    That's a fucking story that moment. And it will never happen
    the same way again. It's fucking unique – Listen t'me, Rich
    – Yer should want t'see that. Take it from me. Things like
    that happen all the time. 'S fucking wonderful.

RICH. Well, next time I go to the Post Office I'll stick my head out of the window. Pete…

Silence.

Please tell me what you've done.

Pause.

PETE. I saved her door till last. Tried everyone I knew before but nothing. No answers, nothing, just nothing. So I drive up that steep hill. Up Crooks. Until I reach her road. And all it is is students. Every house. 'N' I can see them. Sat there. Lounging. Still though I go up to the door. Knock on. 'N' this lad. Twenty. Looks like he fancies himself. Thinks he's got a bit of swagger. Polo shirt. Collar up. Tracksuit. Answers it. He asks me what. 'N' I say where's the woman that lives in this house. 'N' he just laughed at me. Wrong door, mate, wrong door. And went to shut the door. I'm nobody's fucking mate. Certainly not his.

Silence.

RICH. What did you do to yer hand, Pete?

PETE. I.

Silence.

I let him shut the door. Then I walked over to the phone box on the other side of the road and put it through it.

RICH. Right.

PETE. I didn't know what else to do.

Silence.

I don't know anyone else, Rich. It's only that cunt Frank that knows where she'll be.

RICH. Don't speak about him like that.

PETE. Well, that's what he is.

RICH. No he's fucking not! You fucking… Are you surprised?

Silence.

Don't you ask yerself, Pete. Don't yer ask yerself, why would he let you into their lives?

PETE. I'm not asking f'sympathy.

RICH. –

PETE. Just a little chance.

Pause.

I'm not the same as I was.

RICH. Look at yer hand 'n' say that.

Pause.

PETE. When I got in town earlier. When I parked the car. Didn't know where I were. It were like a different place. Roads, shops, everything. So a start walking. Eyes up here. Eventually find meself walkin' along Fargate. 'N' there were no Egg Box. It's gone. Completely gone. Used t'walk past that building. Used t'walk past it and think what a disgrace. Dirty. Oppressive. Bleak piece of shite. So much better now it's gone. Feels fresh. Whole place does. Millennium fucking galleries. Peace gardens. Wannabe City of Culture. Sheffield! Fuck me, this place has been given a second chance. All these fantastic things have fucking happened. Why couldn't I gone in jail during the eighties? Woulda missed nothing.

Beat.

After that I ran down here. I wanted somewhere that didn't seem foreign. Familiar, yer know.

Beat.

All I want is the same chance, yeah?

RICH *looks at* PETE *for a while.*

RICH. Those building didn't just disappear, or appear, Pete. It was a fucking building site for years. Takes time.

Pause.

PETE. You don't realise how important finding her is to me.

RICH. Think I do.

PETE. You don't, Rich. Yer just don't. A don't even have a photo. Not an image. Every girl a see could be her. You'd know yer own child if they walked past, wouldn't yer. Yer'd have that feeling.

Silence.

When I find her.

RICH. What?

PETE. When I…

RICH. What will you do?

Silence.

Are yer sad?

PETE. Course I am.

Silence.

RICH. Come 'n' sit up here.

Pause. He does.

Do yer want t'know somert that makes me sad? I got a girl pregnant.

Pause.

PETE. Come again?

RICH. I got a girl pregnant.

Pause.

We thought it was best that she wasn't.

Pause.

We cried a lot. Was very sad.

Pause.

Very sad indeed.

Pause.

PETE. She leave yer?

RICH. No. After that. Well, it was never the same. She moved away. Moved south. Moved to Chesterfield. Works in a chocolate shop. Lovely girl. Do miss her. But not quite enough, yer know?

Silence.

Anyway, good-looking man like me can't be stuck on the shelf.

PETE. Good-looking man like you?

RICH. Don't doubt it. I'm a stud, me.

PETE. Is that so?

RICH. Yes it is so. In fact, I'm so potent, if I even sneeze near a bird I'll give her an orgasm.

PETE. Now I've heard it all.

RICH. You'd hear even more if you were within a mile radius of the action.

PETE. A mile radius is it?

RICH. Maybe even two miles.

PETE. Is that right.

RICH. Completely right.

PETE. And when was the last time you rocked some poor little raggy doll's world?

Long pause.

RICH. I should text her. Just to say hello.

PETE. Just to say hello?

Silence. RICH *looks away from* PETE. *Silence.*

RICH. Come on. Let's go.

PETE *stares at* RICH. *He then stands and exits with* RICH.

FIVE

A bench outside Notre Dame High School.

PETE *is sat. His hand wrapped in a bandage.*

After a while, MICHELLE *enters. She's a young girl, about fifteen, in school uniform.*

She looks at PETE *for a long time.*

He has no idea what to do. Maybe he covers his hand.

MICHELLE. You like that bench, don't yer.

PETE. Sorry?

MICHELLE. Seen you there loads. You just sit, don't yer? Sit there. Watching us.

PETE. No.

MICHELLE. You do.

Pause.

I should tell the teachers.

PETE. I'll go.

MICHELLE. Get them to come out. Have a word. Maybe call the cops.

PETE. No, no, I'm going.

MICHELLE. 'N' they'll come and take you away. Call you a perv.

PETE. I said I'm going.

MICHELLE. Paedo.

PETE. I'm not.

MICHELLE. Show-off.

PETE. Mean it.

MICHELLE. Yeah.

PETE. Nothing like that at all.

MICHELLE. Yeah.

PETE. Don't keep doing that.

MICHELLE. Prefer it if I went and got the teachers, would you?

PETE. Sorry. Please don't. I'm going. I only wanted to sit here. Think.

MICHELLE. I'm only joking with yer. I ain't going to get them.

PETE *goes to exit.*

Stay. Anyway, look worse won't it if you run off. Like you had done somert wrong.

Pause.

Sit.

Pause.

Sit.

Pause.

Most of the teachers are letches anyway. If they could get away with it, they'd definitely have a go.

Pause.

Shift up then.

PETE. What?

MICHELLE. I don't like standing when I'm talking.

PETE. You want to sit here?

MICHELLE. I can sit on your lap if you'd prefer.

PETE. No, no, no. I should just go. You just –

MICHELLE. I don't bite. Stay.

PETE. Why are you doing this?

MICHELLE. Most men don't normally complain.

PETE. Don't say that.

MICHELLE. True.

PETE. How old are you?

MICHELLE. Old enough.

PETE. Shouldn't you be at school?

MICHELLE. Alright, Dad.

PETE. What?

MICHELLE. Just move up.

Silence. He moves up. She sits. He looks away from her.

What did you do to your hand?

PETE. It's nothing.

MICHELLE. Doesn't look like nothing. Did you hit someone? You did, didn't you? Well, you ain't bandaged it very well. Let me see.

PETE. Don't.

Beat.

Please. Don't.

MICHELLE. Alright, alright, no touching but I ain't an alien, you know. Ain't some sort of monster. Ain't that hard to look at.

PETE. You're anything but a monster. I can't look at yer though.

MICHELLE. Why?

PETE. I just. Can't.

MICHELLE. Right.

Silence.

What's your name?

PETE. I should go.

MICHELLE. Odd name.

PETE *stands.*

Stay. What's yer problem? You ain't done nothing wrong. Just chatting.

PETE. You don't understand.

MICHELLE. What's not to understand?

PETE. I don't know what to say to you.

MICHELLE. Just say your name, that's all I asked.

PETE. I'm not ready for that.

MICHELLE. Not ready for that?

PETE. No. I wasn't prepared for this.

MICHELLE. For what?

PETE. For this. For all this is.

MICHELLE. What?

Pause.

Did nobody tell you it's rude to turn your back on people when they're talking to you?

PETE. Who told you that?

PETE *faces* MICHELLE.

Was it yer mum? Or yer dad?

MICHELLE. Everyone knows that. What aren't you prepared for? All you're telling me is yer name.

Silence.

PETE. My name's Pete.

MICHELLE. Right. Pete.

PETE. Does that mean anything to you?

Pause.

MICHELLE. Peter Andre.

PETE. I'm serious.

MICHELLE. What sort of question is that?

Pause.

You never asked me my name.

PETE. No.

Pause.

MICHELLE. Right. You going to?

PETE. I need you to tell me why you're sat here. I need to know this ain't some sort of joke. That you're not taking the piss out of me.

MICHELLE. I'm not taking the piss. I'm not like that, me.

PETE. Tell me then.

MICHELLE. Why do you sit here, if you ain't looking at kids? It's hardly comfortable.

PETE. Answer me first.

Pause.

MICHELLE. I like going in antique shops. I like looking in windows and spotting things. I like that. I like looking at things that have been used. Loved. Or broken. Chipped. That've got history. I really like that. I think people are very similar. I like looking at people and thinking about what went before. What's given them those knocks and scratches. You've got a very interesting face. Your hand. I think you have lots of stories. I think that.

PETE. Is that the truth?

MICHELLE. Why wouldn't it be?

PETE. You weren't drawn to me?

MICHELLE. What?

PETE. Drawn to me. You recognised me?

MICHELLE. Recognised…

PETE. You weren't looking for me?

MICHELLE. Why would I be looking for you…?

Silence.

Why are you here?

Silence.

PETE. I used to know this girl. Years ago. Before you were born. She went here. She went to this school. She lived here. Round here. We lost touch.

MICHELLE. So you're trying to find her?

PETE. Sort of.

MICHELLE. Just go on Friends Reunited.

PETE. What?

MICHELLE. Don't hang around outside her old school. Fucking hell.

PETE. Did your mum go to this school?

MICHELLE. My mum?

PETE. Yes.

MICHELLE. What's my mum got to do with owt?

PETE. Did she?

MICHELLE. Mighta done.

Pause.

PETE. I've thought about this moment for so long.

MICHELLE. You have?

PETE. Yes, yes I have. I don't think you were telling the truth about why you came and sat here.

MICHELLE. You don't?

PETE. I've sat out here for hours over different days. And nobody's even looked at me. Let alone said hello. And now you. You're sat here. I think you were drawn here.

MICHELLE. Drawn…?

PETE. I think you had a feeling.

MICHELLE. Yeah…

PETE. One that you couldn't answer.

MICHELLE. No.

PETE. And you just came here.

MICHELLE. Yeah.

PETE. And I know why.

MICHELLE. You do?

PETE. Don't be scared of it.

MICHELLE. It's –

PETE. It makes no sense to you, I know. Oh, just look at you.

MICHELLE. Me?

PETE. Look at my face and tell me what you see.

MICHELLE. What I see?

PETE. Yes.

Pause.

MICHELLE. You've got very dark eyes.

PETE. I have, haven't I.

MICHELLE. Yes.

PETE. So have you.

MICHELLE. No I haven't. They're blue.

PETE. Okay. Okay. Look at our hair, we've got the same hair colour.

MICHELLE. This ain't natural. Blonde by birth.

PETE. Right.

MICHELLE. Always changing it. Probably fall out in a few years.

PETE. The shape of our faces.

MICHELLE. Our faces?

PETE. You see it?

MICHELLE. Don't know what I'm looking for.

PETE. Look beyond the physical. Look at me and tell me what you see.

MICHELLE. Why are you doing this?

PETE. I hoped this would be different.

MICHELLE. What would be different?

PETE. Your mum's name's Emma, isn't it?

MICHELLE. Emma?

PETE. Emma Griffin.

MICHELLE. No.

PETE. And you were born on the seventeenth October.

MICHELLE. No.

PETE. At the children's hospital.

MICHELLE. No.

PETE. You weighed seven pounds two ounces.

MICHELLE. No.

PETE. Yes.

MICHELLE. No.

PETE. Yes.

MICHELLE. No.

PETE. Yes, you're –

MICHELLE. Stop this, stop this. I wasn't drawn here. I had a bet with my friends. That's why I came here. They said I wouldn't dare talk to you.

Pause.

They owe me twenty quid.

Pause.

They were going to take pictures on their phones. Post it on Bebo.

PETE. Right, right. I don't even know what that is but right.

MICHELLE. I've only lived in Sheffield since I was seven. My mum's called Jackie. She grew up in Nottingham.

Silence.

PETE. Sorry. I'm so sorry. I don't know what I've done.

Pause.

I thought you could be.

Pause.

I don't know what I thought.

Pause.

I wanted to believe.

Pause.

I don't know what she looks like. Sorry.

MICHELLE. Pete.

PETE. She could be –

MICHELLE. Pete.

PETE. Yeah?

MICHELLE. I'm the one that should be sorry.

PETE. Don't be. I was stupid. Am stupid.

MICHELLE. I thought you were just a weirdo. Liked buses or something like that.

PETE. I don't like buses.

Pause.

Are they watching?

MICHELLE. Yes.

PETE. You should go and get your twenty quid.

MICHELLE *stands.* PETE *looks away. Long pause.*

MICHELLE. Do you want to talk to me?

Pause.

PETE. What?

MICHELLE. Do you want to talk to me? You'll know I'll be lying but you can ask me questions.

PETE. Yeah?

MICHELLE. Ask me them as if I was drawn here.

PETE. Really?

MICHELLE. Yeah.

Beat.

You have earned me twenty quid.

Silence.

PETE. Okay. Okay. Yes, okay.

MICHELLE. I'll sit.

PETE. Okay.

She does.

Silence.

What's your name?

MICHELLE. Michelle.

PETE. Can I call you Elizabeth instead? Can that be your name? Lizzie or Liz.

MICHELLE. Okay.

Pause.

PETE. Lizzie.

Pause.

I'm Pete.

Pause.

Hi.

MICHELLE. Hi.

PETE. I'm. I'm your.

Pause.

But you can call me, call me whatever's easiest. If you're not comfortable with calling me... just call me Pete, whichever...

MICHELLE. Okay.

Pause.

PETE. I've got so many things I wanted to tell, ask, you. But. Look at you.

Pause.

So grown up. You're lucky you take after your mother more than me.

Pause.

How's school?

MICHELLE. It's good.

PETE. Good. Good. Good. That's good.

Pause.

What, what, what's your favorite subject...? Is it English?

MICHELLE. Yeah.

PETE. I thought it would be. Knew that. Is that because of Shakespeare?

MICHELLE. Yeah.

PETE. And I bet you've already started thinking about university, haven't you?

MICHELLE. Yeah.

PETE. And all those things you're going to learn.

MICHELLE. Yeah.

PETE. And that future you're going to have…

MICHELLE. That's right.

PETE. That fills me up that does.

MICHELLE. Good. That's good.

PETE. Are you scared of the dark?

MICHELLE. What do you think?

PETE. I think you are.

MICHELLE. Well, that's right. I am.

PETE. It's okay. We're all scared of things.

MICHELLE. Thank you.

PETE. Just look at you…

Lights have by now faded to black.

SIX

Outside (LUCY*'s mum*), MAGGIE ASHTON*'s house.*

MAGGIE. A hoped I'd never see you again.

RICH. Mrs Ashton.

MAGGIE. What d'yer want?

RICH. I want t'see her. Got somert for her. A want t'give it to her.

MAGGIE. She won't want it.

RICH. Please let me see her.

MAGGIE. No.

RICH. You hate me.

MAGGIE. That a question.

RICH. No, I know the answer.

MAGGIE. Well, just in case yer not sure, to erase any confusion: the answer's yes.

RICH. 'N' I understand that.

MAGGIE. Well then go.

RICH. A can't.

MAGGIE. If yer care about her at all, yer will.

Pause.

She tells me everything, yer know.

RICH. Right.

MAGGIE. You ripped her life in two.

Pause.

RICH. A need t'see her.

MAGGIE. No.

RICH. Please.

MAGGIE. No.

RICH. Do yer miss her?

MAGGIE. What?

RICH. Now that she's moved out.

MAGGIE. She weren't ready t'leave. She needed carin'. You forced her.

RICH. No.

MAGGIE. She couldn't bear t'be near you. After what you. You, as if nothin' happened. Yer drove her from her own home. Her own mother. You drove my little girl away.

Silence.

RICH. Saw you through the window before a knocked on.

MAGGIE. Yer shouldn't pry.

RICH. Yer looked different. Used t'think you had a right old sour-face. But I just realised it's because you love her so much, don't yer.

MAGGIE. Every single bit of her.

RICH. 'N' yer used t'look like that because you knew I was wrong. Your way of guarding her. 'N' that made me realise that love can make yer look funny. Like with all that hate you had f'me. Distorted you. Cos you've got such a kind face.

MAGGIE. You were never good enough for her.

RICH. No.

MAGGIE. What she saw in you I will never know.

RICH. She said it were my eyes.

MAGGIE. And do you know what?

RICH. What?

MAGGIE. It's best that it happened. Because you would have been an awful father. Dad. 'S genetic.

RICH. Don't.

MAGGIE. Would just have ended up abandoning both of them. Like your dad did.

RICH. Stop.

MAGGIE. And your brother has.

RICH. I am nothing like that person. Or my brother. Alright, nothing.

Silence.

She doesn't tell you everything, does she? Otherwise you would never have said that. However much you...

Silence.

I told you that you had a kind face.

MAGGIE. Richard.

RICH. I saw you through the window and you had such a kind face.

MAGGIE. She's my daughter. The things that can make you do. One day you may understand.

Silence.

RICH. She looked healthy.

MAGGIE. She's put weight on.

RICH. Yeah.

MAGGIE. It makes her cheeks glow more.

RICH. I were so proud of her.

MAGGIE. Pardon?

RICH. She has such delicate hands. The way she wrapped those chocolates. Despite me being… Such a skill. I… I wish…

MAGGIE. What?

RICH. A wish I'd told my mum.

MAGGIE. You're a confused little boy.

RICH. Probably.

Silence.

MAGGIE. What do you want to say to her?

RICH. Mrs Ashton.

MAGGIE. It's a simple question, Richard.

RICH. It's between me and her.

MAGGIE. She only needs one thing from yer.

RICH. I got her something.

MAGGIE. No, she doesn't need that.

RICH. You don't know what it is.

MAGGIE. Richard. You know what she needs from you, don't you.

Pause.

Don't you?

RICH. Yes.

MAGGIE. Say it then.

RICH. Please can I see her.

MAGGIE. If you can't say it to me then you won't be able to say it to her.

RICH. I will.

MAGGIE. I don't trust you.

Silence.

She's not going to absorb your guilt for you.

RICH. You're not going to let me see her, are you?

MAGGIE. So simple to rectify.

RICH. Your face is changing. Soft lines are going.

MAGGIE. You surprised?

RICH. Like a gargoyle guarding the gate.

MAGGIE. I've only entertained you because I thought yer might have come t'put an end to her hurting. But you haven't. So you should go.

RICH. Will you give her these.

MAGGIE. No

RICH. –

MAGGIE. Go on. Go.

RICH. –

MAGGIE. Walk away, little boy.

> RICH *stares at her.* RICH *offers her the bag. She doesn't take it.* RICH *then forces the bag into her hand.*

What you doing?

RICH. Take them.

> RICH *forces her to take them. A moment.*

I'm a good person. Don't try and paint me as anything different. It's not fair. We've all got flaws.

MAGGIE. –

RICH. You give her them.

Silence.

MAGGIE. 'N' you said you were different.

> RICH *starts to shake, aware of what he has just done. He can't look* MAGGIE *in the face. He exits quickly.* MAGGIE *goes back into the house. We see* LUCY *in the window, she watches* MAGGIE *as she drops the bag into a wheelie bin and then goes back into the house.*

SEVEN

*FRANK's house. Model aeroplanes hang from the ceiling.
FRANK is sat on a chair in front of a table, at which he is
working on another plane. The only other item of interest in the
room is a framed picture of RICH. Eventually there is a knock
at the door. FRANK looks at his watch. Puts his glasses on.
Goes to the door. PETE is there. He is wearing a shirt and his
right hand is bandaged.*

Eventually...

FRANK. You.

PETE. Yes.

Silence.

FRANK (*re: hand*). They say a leopard never changes its spots.

PETE. It was a window.

Pause.

FRANK. A shirt. Very –

PETE. Rich... said I should wear it. Makes me more presentable.

FRANK. 'E knows you're here?

PETE. No. We need t'talk.

FRANK. We?

Silence.

PETE. Will you let me in?

FRANK. Do I have a choice?

Silence.

Take your shoes off.

PETE. My shoes?

FRANK. Leave your shoes at the door. Least pay me that small
respect.

*FRANK goes back into the room. PETE takes his shoes off.
PETE then follows FRANK in. FRANK has positioned
himself so the table is between them.*

Well, isn't this a pleasant surprise.

PETE. Really?

FRANK. No. What d'yer want?

PETE. –

FRANK. You're wasting your time.

PETE *looks round the room.*

PETE. Bit empty this place.

FRANK. Yes. Yes it is.

PETE. You made all these?

FRANK. And more.

PETE. They're beautiful.

Silence. PETE *goes over to the table. Looks at the plane* FRANK *is assembling.*

FRANK. Don't.

Beat.

Don't.

PETE *steps back.*

How's Rich?

PETE. He's. Actually I don't know. I don't know what good or bad is in his world.

FRANK. He doesn't talk to me as much any more. Or visit.

PETE. No?

FRANK. Still got a present f'him. From his birthday.

PETE. September.

FRANK. Well done. Nigh on two month.

PETE. I want to thank you.

FRANK. What?

PETE. For looking out for him. For doing that. What?

FRANK. I don't want your thanks. I don't need your thanks! Do you think that means anything to me?

PETE *steps forward.*

PETE. Frank.

FRANK. I did it because I wanted to. For him.

PETE. Don't shout, Frank.

FRANK. STAY WHERE YOU ARE.

Long pause.

That was me shouting.

PETE. Yes.

FRANK. This is my house.

PETE. Yes.

FRANK. Don't tell me what I can't do in my own house.

Silence.

Now I need some water.

FRANK *exits.* FRANK *returns with two glasses of water. He puts one on the table for* PETE. PETE *goes to say thanks,* FRANK *looks at him, he doesn't. They drink. They look at each other.*

Eventually…

PETE. What did yer get him?

FRANK. Rich?

PETE. For his birthday.

FRANK *looks away, decides he will tell* PETE.

FRANK. An Xbox.

PETE. A what?

FRANK. It's a computer console.

PETE. Right.

Beat.

I could pass it on to him. If yer not going t'see him.

FRANK. I don't think so.

PETE. Frank.

FRANK. –

PETE. Frank. Frank.

FRANK. Pete.

PETE. Do you send my daughter presents?

FRANK. Yer using that word again.

PETE. Do you?

FRANK. Do I?

PETE. I'm sure you do. Way you were with Emma. Way you. Supported. Why was that?

FRANK. Because she was a nice girl. Who didn't deserve –

PETE. It were none a yer business.

FRANK. Felt responsible.

PETE. Yer weren't my fucking dad!

FRANK. No. No, I wasn't. I'm definitely not your dad. But. I.

Long pause.

PETE. Do you?

Long pause.

FRANK. It's a horrible place, int it?

PETE. What?

FRANK. Prison.

PETE. You?

FRANK. I hurt someone. I was very young. And stupid. Luckily they caught me.

PETE. Is that why you came?

FRANK. Who knows now. Maybe I wanted to let you know you ruined my life. And that you'll never sleep properly again. Or I could have come to warn you that there's always someone bigger. And that you should keep your mouth shut. I just don't remember now.

FRANK *drinks some of his water.*

PETE. You're the only one that came yer know. After all I did. I shoulda seen yer.

FRANK. Maybe. Yer mum never visited?

PETE. No.

FRANK. She really gave you up in the end.

PETE. Couple years too late f'you.

FRANK. Maybe.

Silence.

PETE. You miss my mum?

FRANK. Don't.

PETE. You never? After? Nothing else?

FRANK. There were times. A couple. When I thought. No.

PETE. What's her new bloke like?

FRANK. Can you not.

PETE. Frank.

FRANK. Don't know. But I hope he's a fucking lovely man because she deserves that.

FRANK *finishes off his water. Fiddles with the glass.*

PETE. So this is what you do?

FRANK. They keep me busy.

PETE. What is it, yer just put 'em together?

FRANK. No.

PETE. Because that would be quite simple, wouldn't it?

FRANK. Every piece. Every little bit 'as t'be shaped. Has to be measured. Painted. It's… rewarding.

PETE. Can imagine.

FRANK. Can you? You were always so much more capable of taking things apart than putting them back together.

PETE. I got a BTEC in Woodwork.

FRANK. What?

PETE. Studied it. Tried my hand at lots of things. They're very up for rehabilitation. Liked plumbing most. But most of the time all I did was think.

PETE *picks up the model aeroplane.*

Never worked on anything so delicate before.

Silence.

FRANK. Will yer put that down.

Long pause. PETE *does.*

PETE. I need to find her, Frank.

FRANK. What good will it do? Biology, blood or DNA means nothing in this case, science doesn't tell you the whole picture, cos you ain't her father. You ain't. Be honest with yerself.

Silence.

PETE. I need to find her, Frank.

FRANK. No.

PETE. Frank.

FRANK. ...No.

PETE. Frank.

FRANK. Why?

PETE. I met. This girl.

FRANK. A girl?

PETE. Yes.

FRANK. You mean a woman? Like an older woman.

PETE. No. I wanted so badly for it to be her.

FRANK. No, no, Pete. Don't, I don't want to believe this.

PETE. I really did.

FRANK. What did you do?

PETE. I spoke to her.

FRANK. ...You?

PETE. I spoke to her.

FRANK. That's all? What did you say?

PETE. I realised what it was all about. Why I need to find her. I asked her all the things I hoped she'd be. I asked her everything that would make her different to me. I need to know that it's true.

Silence.

FRANK. Is that the truth?

PETE. Frank.

FRANK. Are you sorry?

PETE. Sometimes it's impossible to explain exactly how we feel. We'd need to invent new words to do so. But I ain't got an original bone in my body.

Silence.

FRANK. Are you sorry?

PETE. Every second. Every single second.

Silence.

She...

Silence.

Don't stop me finding this out. I mean it, Frank. I really mean it. I need to know this too much.

Pause.

FRANK. You want t'know why I came?

PETE. Tell me.

FRANK. I wanted to say sorry.

PETE. To me?

FRANK. I wanted to apologise. I wanted to say I'm sorry for not stopping you. I could have. If I hadn't told them it was an accident. If I told them you'd done it deliberately. Like you did. That I didn't slip. That you did do it. Thought I was doing what was best for you... Thought, thought you'd learn... Thought...

PETE. Show me. Show me.

FRANK *takes his shirt off. Across his back are three large scars. They have the space between them of the points from a garden fork.* PETE *looks at* FRANK*'s back.*

Eventually...

...I did this...

FRANK. This could have stopped you. If I had. You would never. I could have sent you there years before. Your mum would have. And you wouldn't be asking what you're. Learnt earlier. Coulda, shoulda...

PETE. I wish you had. I wish you fucking had.

PETE *has hold of* FRANK*'s face. He stares at him for a long, long time.*

You owe me. You owe me...

Eventually...

FRANK. Address book. In the kitchen. Drawer next to the fridge.

PETE *stares at* FRANK, *lets him go.*

PETE *exits to the kitchen.*

FRANK *tries to gather his thoughts.*

A knock at the door.

FRANK *ignores it.*

Another more aggressive knock.

From off, we hear RICH.

RICH. Frank?

FRANK *recognises the voice. He quickly puts his shirt back on. Goes to the door.*

FRANK. Rich?

RICH. Can I come in?

FRANK....Course. Course you can.

RICH. What?

FRANK. No it's fine. Come in. Come in.

RICH *goes to take off his shoes*.

Don't worry about your shoes.

RICH. Don't let me take short cuts, Frank.

FRANK. Alright, take them off.

RICH *takes his shoes off. He enters the room.* FRANK *follows him.*

What's this about, Rich?

RICH. Frank, I've let you down.

FRANK. What?

RICH. You were so good to me.

FRANK. Slow down. Tell me what you've done.

RICH. Didn't think I was like him.

FRANK. Like who?

RICH. Pete. Is it like osmosis, Frank, is it just absorbing into me by being close to him?

FRANK. Is what? Richard?

RICH. I went to see Lucy. But her mum wouldn't let me see her. And so I grabbed her arms and I hurt her. It wasn't for long, Frank, it was just a burst. This urge.

FRANK. Rich.

RICH. Just flooded through me. Fucking... Frank, are you listening to what I'm saying?

FRANK. Course I am.

RICH. Because you promised me that you'd always be there for me.

FRANK. I know I did.

RICH. You promised that and right now you seem to be very distracted.

FRANK. I'm sorry.

RICH. I need you right now, Frank.

FRANK. I know you do.

RICH. Then what is it?

FRANK. Alright. Okay, you need to know.

RICH. What?

FRANK. Yer brother's here, Rich.

RICH. What?

FRANK. Pete… is in the house.

RICH. I don't understand.

FRANK. I didn't want you to talk about him with him only
being in there.

> PETE *enters. He stares at* RICH.

RICH. You shouldn't be here.

FRANK. It's okay.

RICH. No it's not. What have you done to him?

FRANK. He's done nothing.

RICH. I don't believe you.

PETE. Because I'm not capable of anything else, am I?

RICH. What?

PETE. These walls aren't half thin.

RICH. You heard what I was saying?

PETE. Sounds like it's you that's acting out of order.

RICH. And whose fault is that?

FRANK. Boys.

RICH. We're not boys, Frank!

FRANK. I won't have you arguing.

RICH. He needs to hear this.

PETE. Let him speak, Frank. Say it.

RICH. I've never done anything like this before. And you
arrive. And suddenly…

PETE. My fault, is it?

RICH. Where else does it come from?

FRANK. Stay where you both are.

PETE. No, let him come at me.

RICH. Yer just a slug. The fucking trail you leave.

FRANK. Stop this.

PETE. No, let him fucking finish, Frank.

RICH. I should never have let you in the front door.

PETE. Is that right?

RICH. I should have used it as a battering ram instead.

PETE. Did you enjoy it?

RICH. What?

PETE. When you did that, when you grabbed her, did you enjoy it? Tell me if you enjoyed it.

RICH. ...Frank.

FRANK. Richard, did you?

RICH. I don't know.

PETE. That's not good enough. Yes or no.

FRANK. Don't touch him.

PETE. Stay out of this. This is between me and him.

PETE *has grabbed hold of* RICH*'s arms.*

If you're going to blame me then give me an answer.

Silence.

Did you?

FRANK. Yer scaring him.

PETE. No, I'm getting through to him. Would you go back and do it again?

RICH. No. No. No, Pete, I wouldn't.

PETE *grasps* RICH*'s face, eventually he looks at him with all the tenderness he can muster.*

PETE. Yer nothing like me.

RICH *nods.* PETE *lets go.*

Yer a soft lad. Don't ever forget that.

PETE *has to find a way to calm himself down. He paces. Shakes his head violently. Picks up an aeroplane. Puts it down. Rubs his face.*

FRANK. Pete.

PETE. Let me be.

Pause.

I need this to pass.

PETE *gathers himself together. Eventually.*

RICH. Have you ever buried something so deep inside you forgot how to let it out?

PETE. What do you think?

FRANK. What's this about?

PETE. He got her pregnant, didn't he.

FRANK. Lucy?

PETE. She's not any more.

FRANK. I see.

RICH. I should have told you. I should have spoken to you. But I didn't. I didn't tell anyone. He was the first… I wasn't good to her, Frank. I wasn't… I just wish, wish that she'd say it's okay… I want to be the person that did the right thing… I want to be… that… but… but I'm just… just not…

FRANK. Come on, sit down.

RICH *sits down.*

Pete. Would yer get yer brother some water?

PETE. Okay.

PETE *exits.*

RICH. I forgot how beautiful these planes are.

FRANK. Richard.

RICH. Yes?

FRANK. Don't ever go thinking you've let me down. Whenever I think about you, whenever I see you, all I feel is pride.

RICH. Thank you.

FRANK. Yer don't have to thank me. But you know what you've got to do, don't you. It's as much for you as it is for her.

RICH *nods*.

RICH. Are you okay?

FRANK. Me?

RICH. Why's he here?

FRANK. I'm okay. That's all you need to know.

RICH. Did you tell him where she lives? Frank? Is that wise?

FRANK. I can't be the obstacle for him. I'm trusting that he will make the right decision. I owe him that much.

RICH. You've done more for this family than it ever deserved.

FRANK. Well, that's kind of you to say.

RICH. No, Frank, it's just the truth.

PETE *re-enters. He gives* RICH *the glass of water.*

I didn't mean that about you being a slug.

PETE. It's okay. I know what I am.

A knock at the door.

RICH. You expecting someone?

FRANK. Me? You do flatter me. Probably Jehovah's.

FRANK *goes to the door. He opens it.* LUCY *is at the door, she has a set of photographs in her hand.*

LUCY. Hello, Frank.

FRANK. Lucy. I thought you might be a Jehovah's Witness. Knocking at the door. Out of the blue like this.

LUCY. Is it out of the blue?

FRANK. It's not me you came here to talk to, is it.

LUCY. Talk?

FRANK. That's my polite way of saying confront. Come in. Freezing out there. Don't worry about your shoes.

LUCY. Yer a nice man, Frank.

LUCY *enters the room.*

RICH. Luce?

LUCY. What is wrong with you?

RICH. What are you doing here?

LUCY. What am I doing here? Have you any idea what you've just done?

RICH. Yes.

LUCY. Then how can you ask me that.

RICH. But – here.

LUCY. I know you, if that's what you're getting at. I guessed where you'd come.

LUCY *notices* PETE.

Who are you?

RICH. This is Pete.

LUCY. Yer brother?

Silence.

You don't look alike.

PETE. Is that a good thing?

LUCY. It's just an observation.

PETE. He told me about you.

LUCY. Wonder how real that story was.

RICH. I told him the truth.

LUCY. What is this – happy families?

RICH. Look, you're angry with me.

LUCY. Anger doesn't begin to describe it.

RICH. Shall we go for a walk?

LUCY. Yer joking.

RICH. Get some fresh air. Talk about it outside.

LUCY. No.

RICH. No?

LUCY. No, Rich. I came here.

RICH. This is not the place.

LUCY. Different, is it then, when it's not on your terms? Typical.

RICH. This is Frank's house, Lucy.

LUCY. I am well aware of that.

RICH. Yer wearing yer shoes.

FRANK. Richard, I said it was fine.

LUCY. Why are you staring at me?

PETE. It doesn't look natural on you.

LUCY. What?

RICH. Pete, please don't say owt.

PETE. Anger. The faces you're pulling. Doesn't suit you.

LUCY. Most people say I brighten up their day.

PETE. I bet they do. He's pushed you a long way, hasn't he?

LUCY. He just dunt know when to stop.

PETE. We're not very good with words in our family.

LUCY. Actions speak louder, isn't it.

Silence.

PETE. Perhaps we should give you two a minute.

FRANK. We'll be in the back.

PETE *and* FRANK *exit.* LUCY *and* RICH *stare at each other.*

RICH. Did you like the photographs?

LUCY. Rich.

RICH. I didn't even remember taking them.

LUCY. You think they're things I want?

RICH. We looked so happy.

LUCY. Don't.

RICH. Looked so much younger as well. Only year ago.

LUCY. Cos nothing had happened yet.

RICH. Remember thinking how wise we were. One year, I feel so much more –

LUCY *throws the photographs at* RICH.

Careful. Planes. The...

LUCY. This isn't about you!

Silence.

RICH. I didn't mean to do that with your mum.

LUCY. You grabbed her.

RICH. I know what I did.

LUCY. She's got marks on her arms.

RICH. I don't know what happened. I can't explain it.

LUCY. That's the worse explanation I've ever heard.

RICH. Please don't hold that against me. That's not what I'm like. You know that. You know that's not me.

LUCY. Don't try and turn the tables.

RICH. I'm not.

LUCY. You are. That's all you've ever done. Fucking well accept what you've done.

Silence.

I don't believe you. What did I ever see in you?

RICH. Lots and lots of things.

LUCY. Don't look at me.

RICH. Luce –

LUCY. I can't believe I'm stood here doing this. It's not fair. I was doing it, yer know, getting over this, over you, I really was. Then you. You keep interfering with my. I even went on a date. He was so nice. D'yer want t'know his name?

RICH. No.

LUCY. It was Simon. And he was... My mum would have liked him. But because you're back. Trudging. I could be happy. I could meet people like him. Let me be. What?

RICH. Happy. I'm pleased f'yer. That you could –

LUCY. Fuck off.

RICH *goes to put his hand down his trousers.*

Don't do that. 'S disgusting.

Silence.

You and your brother seem t'be getting on well.

RICH. He's alright, really.

LUCY. Well, most people who have killed people are.

RICH. 'E knows where 'is daughter is.

LUCY. You know I thought of all the people, you'd tell him t'let her be. Let her get on with her life.

RICH. Needs to do it.

LUCY. There you go. Stop thinking about yerselves. Think about others involved. Acting all gung-ho as if you've been aggrieved. You. He. Both. That's what you're both doing.

RICH. Keep your voice down.

LUCY. I don't care. Yer just selfish. Not thinking about anyone else's feelings.

RICH. Yer don't understand.

LUCY. Would you want your dad turning up out of the blue?

RICH. That's different. It is. It is.

LUCY. It was so cold. On that trolley. Waiting to go in. On my back. You can't appreciate that. You can't appreciate what I had to go through. And I think that every time I see you. I think about how cold it was. How lonely I was because that's the only way I can see you now –

RICH. I'm sorry.

LUCY. What?

RICH. I am so, so, so sorry.

Silence.

So if you never want to see me again, just say so now and I'll let you be.

Long pause.

LUCY. Goodbye, Richard.

LUCY *exits.* RICH *picks up the photographs.* FRANK *and* PETE *enter.*

RICH. You heard that?

FRANK. Let me take these off yer.

FRANK *takes the photographs off* RICH. *He gestures him to sit down.* RICH *sits. They sit next to him. Eventually,* RICH *starts to smile. They share a moment together before the lights fade.*

EIGHT

That morning. Four o'clock. PETE *is sat in* RICH*'s car. A quiet residential street in Cottingham, Hull. Rain is falling heavily outside.* PETE *is staring at a house, on the opposite side of the road. He is chewing intently. A light comes on in the house.* PETE *moves about in his seat.* PETE *gets out of the car. Throws his chewing gum aside.* PETE *waits, oblivious to the rain.* TONY *enters, he is a much smaller man than* PETE *and wears glasses. They stand facing each other.*

Eventually…

TONY. Not cricket weather, is it? Game would definitely be called off. Abandoned. Not that you play cricket at night. Not a fan?

PETE. No.

TONY. Well, that's good. Most people just started saying they were after the Ashes. Didn't even know the rules.

PETE. I don't know the rules.

TONY. No. No. No, why would you.

Long pause.

Hello.

Long pause.

We've never met.

PETE. I know who you are.

TONY. I'd like you to call me Tony.

Pause.

Pete, I'd like you to call me Tony. Pete?

PETE. Icy roads.

TONY. Yeah. Sorry?

PETE. Coming down the roads were dead icy. These tyres don't have much tread either. Virtually crawled here. Speed I was going at.

TONY. The gritters should have been out.

PETE. They had.

TONY. Never get stuck behind one. Makes your car look like it's been pebble-dashed.

PETE. Bear that in mind.

TONY. Although it looks like it already has. Sorry. No offence. It's a nice car.

PETE. It's a pile of shite. Fucking rust.

Pause.

No tread.

TONY. Thought you might have come here for a fight.

PETE. Not sure why I've come.

TONY. That's why I put my glasses on. You could never hit a man in glasses. Could you?

PETE. No.

Pause.

Take them off.

Pause.

TONY. I'm not sure if that's a joke or not.

PETE. Neither am I.

Pause.

TONY. I bet you've got lots of questions you'd like to ask me.

PETE. Yeah. Yeah. Yeah.

TONY. Shall we sit in the car?

PETE. Yeah. Careful though the...

TONY. What?

PETE. Gotta be...

TONY. Yes?

PETE. The door's... fucked.

TONY. Right.

PETE. 'Ave t'yank it. Gets jarred.

TONY. Right.

> TONY *goes to do it. The door is jarred.*

> Not joking.

PETE. Don't be...

TONY. It is alright to really pull it?

PETE. There's a technique. Let me.

TONY. You...

PETE. I'll. It's...

> PETE *yanks the door open. He goes back round to the driver's side.*

> *They sit in the two front seats.*

> *Long pause.*

TONY. Before we do this –

PETE. Street seems nice. Was thinking that as I was sat here. Thinking how nice it looked. How peaceful and quiet.

TONY. It's four in the morning.

PETE. Must be good f'families.

TONY. We're a very lucky family. Very happy.

PETE *looks out of the window, away from* TONY.

PETE. Suppose yer work really hard. T'get a place like this yer must 'ave t'work really 'ard. Important job.

TONY. Pete, why are you here?

PETE. What job d'yer do? I think it must be a really good job.

TONY. What I do doesn't matter.

PETE *turns to face* TONY.

PETE. D'yer not think I 'ave a right t'know?

TONY. No. No I don't.

Silence.

Frank warned us.

PETE. Warned?

TONY. Let us know that you were back. That you were looking. He cares so much for Jenny. He is –

PETE. Jenny?

TONY. Yes. Frank's a remarkable / man.

PETE. She's called Jenny.

TONY. You didn't know?

PETE. Nobody would let me know.

TONY. I assumed you knew.

PETE. In my head I always thought that she would be called Elizabeth.

TONY. Well, my daughter's name is Jenny.

Pause.

Emma christened her Jennifer. But, well, she's at that age where she's more likely to scratch your eyes out than respond to Jennifer.

Pause.

So it's Jenny. Or Jen. She doesn't mind Jen.

Silence.

PETE. Somert soothing about sitting in a car. Rain coming down.

TONY. Is there?

PETE. Makes me feel dead, dead secure. Always feel safe.

TONY. I'm feeling a little claustrophobic if I'm being honest.

PETE. Yer can wind down your seat.

TONY. No.

PETE. Lie back.

TONY. No.

PETE. Look out of the roof. Dead easy. Just.

TONY. I'll open the window.

PETE. Alright.

TONY *winds down the window a little.*

TONY. I don't have long, Pete.

PETE. Right.

TONY. Emma will guess I'm not in the bathroom.

PETE. She doesn't know you're out here?

TONY. I got up for a glass of water. Is this the first time you've been here?

PETE. Yes.

TONY. Not sat out here all night before?

PETE. No. D'yer know it's sixty-five miles door to door?

TONY. Please don't say things like that. Ask me a question.

PETE. Do you like Hull?

TONY. Not about me.

PETE. Because I always thought Nick Barmby was a bit of a cunt.

TONY. I'm from Hertfordshire originally.

PETE. Where?

TONY. Near Watford.

PETE. Elton John. Need I –

TONY. You have a chance to ask me questions about Jennifer. I will go.

> TONY *looks at* PETE. PETE *doesn't respond.* TONY *goes to exit.*

PETE. Darryl Jones.

TONY. What?

PETE. Scouse lad. We shared a cell. He had three kids. Loved them rotten. One day we were just sat. Sat on our bunks and he doubles up in pain. Lasts a couple of seconds. Intense bolt. And he goes t'me somert's wrong. One of me kids is hurt. I think, fuck that. Indigestion. Used t'wolf 'is food down. Turns out his three-year-old got hit by a car that day. Broke one of its legs and hip. Blew me away.

TONY. I'm going to go, Pete.

> PETE *gently places his arm on* TONY, *without stopping his story.*

PETE. Then. So. About a year ago. I'm sat. Sat in the library and I get this. My whole body tenses. Agony. Clasping my chest. Can barely breathe. Last no more than five seconds. But. Well. What I wanted to know. Did. Last year. Was there an accident? Did she get injured? Or?

TONY. No.

PETE. Was in March.

TONY. No.

PETE. March fifteenth.

TONY. No.

PETE. You coulda forgotten. It was in the afternoon.

TONY. Jenny has never broken a bone. Or injured. She's never been seriously or even minorly injured. Thank God.

PETE. Right, right, right. Right.

Pause.

Right, I don't know what I wanted you to say then.

TONY. You should get that checked out. Sounds like a heart problem.

Pause.

PETE. Sometimes it's okay to be cruel. If that's what you want.

TONY. It's time I went.

PETE. I'd like you to stay.

TONY. Please don't say that.

PETE. I do.

TONY. I should have stayed indoors. I just wanted to say something to you. Adrenalin took over.

PETE. Say it.

TONY. Now it's all gone. And I'm, I'm just remembering how I hate confrontations.

PETE. Nobody does like them.

TONY. But I really don't. Really, really don't. We're quite. We're very different. God's sake, you've killed a man. I feel guilty pruning roses.

Pause.

Sorry. You don't need reminding. I'm sure.

PETE. What did you want to say?

TONY. I have to go.

PETE. Tony.

TONY. I'll wind up the window.

PETE. Stay.

TONY. You should go home. I am.

PETE. Please.

TONY *tries to open the door. Gives it a good push.*

TONY. If this door…

PETE. What's she scared of?

TONY *waits.*

TONY. Pardon?

PETE. Does she get scared of things? Is she scared of the dark?

TONY. No. No, she's not scared of the dark.

PETE. I used t'be.

TONY. She's not.

PETE. Does she like it when it rains?

TONY. Only when it's with thunder.

PETE. She should play in the rain. Playing in the rain is –

TONY. Pete.

PETE. I want to know what makes her smile.

TONY. This is –

PETE. Shut the door and tell me what makes her smile.

TONY *waits. Shuts the door.*

TONY. She's a teenager. I don't know what makes her smile at the moment.

PETE. Well, you should.

TONY. She's…!

Beat.

When the dog snores she laughs. On her rollerskates. Watching *The OC*. Finding odd-shaped potatoes in the supermarket. Me swearing. Hull FC. Some handsome actors. Brad Pitt. Ring tone on her phone. Her friends. Lots of things make her smile. Lots and lots of things.

PETE. D'yer know what made me smile the other day?

TONY. No.

PETE. My brother used to tell people that I was dead. Thought that was funny. Then I realised he was being serious.

Pause.

I'm not dead. Or missing. Not absent. I'm contactable. Have a mobile fucking phone. And I'm here.

TONY. Yes you are.

PETE. Does she look like me?

Pause.

TONY. She's got blonde hair. Just past her shoulder. Often wears it tied up. People would say that she's average height but I think that does her an injustice as she's the perfect height for her features. Bright-blue eyes. Really bright and clear. Nose, well, at the moment, she's claiming that she's going to get a 'nose job' when she's eighteen. I think. I'm sure she'll change her mind. She's very pretty. I'm sure she breaks lots of hearts. I dread her going out clubbing.

PETE. Does she look like me?

TONY. I'm an accountant. A very good one. Figures, numbers, fascinate me. I'm addicted to sudoku. Numbers. You know where you are with numbers. They don't change. I like that. I like knowing that certain things don't change. See language. Language is always evolving. No better proof of that is having a teenager. Sometimes I don't understand a word she says.

PETE. Does she look like me?

TONY. I'm good at my job. Not because of intelligence. But because I work hard. Hours a day. All the extra reading to stay ahead of the game, I do. And I enjoy it. I'm a bit 'geeky'. Jenny, she's like me. Not naturally the most intelligent. But she has such drive. Works so hard. Wants to learn more and more. That's why she's going to be so successful in whatever she chooses.

We have the same ethic.

We are so similar in the way we think.

Way we act.

And this is what I wanted to tell you. She knows nothing about you.

Nothing.

We think that's for the best.

Pause.

She calls me Dad. She is my daughter.

Very long pause.

PETE. Of course, course, course. Course. Yeah. Yeah. I –

TONY. I love her with every fibre. Every. There's nothing. I look at her and I see Emma and me. I see our daughter.

Long pause.

PETE. These fucking seats can be so uncomfortable, can't they.

TONY. If you have something you'd like me to keep for her. When she's eighteen. She can decide if she wants to. I'll let you do that. But she's never asked about you. Let me make that clear.

Silence.

You won't come back. Deep down you know that's the right thing.

TONY *goes to exit but the door jars.*

This fucking door.

PETE *starts to laugh.*

What?

PETE *continues to laugh. He can't stop himself.* TONY *has managed to force the door open.*

What? What?

PETE. You sounded like a right prick when you swore.

PETE *continues to laugh uncontrollably.*

TONY *watches for a second then shuts the door.*

TONY *exits.*

PETE *continues to laugh.*

PETE*'s laughter changes. It's no longer amusing.*

Puts his head in his hands.

His head on the steering wheel.

Fade, as PETE*'s noises become more silent and uncontrollable.*

NINE

Two days later. Afternoon. Living room. PETE *has his small bag packed by his feet. He looks round the room. Sound of the front door opening. He moves the bag so that it is not clearly visible.* RICH *enters with a plastic shopping bag.*

RICH. Alright?

No response.

Yer look like one of them statues. Frozen. Do yer move when I put some money by yer feet?

RICH *makes a gesture to indicate a movement.*

Obviously not. Just as well, I ain't got any change.

PETE. Rich.

RICH. Yeah?

PETE. Will yer sit down.

RICH *notices the bag. Beat.*

RICH. Pete?

PETE. Please.

Long pause.

RICH. Can I show yer somert first. Please.

PETE. Okay.

RICH. I got somert f'you.

PETE. F'me?

RICH. Yeah. But before you say anything I want t'make it clear – it was a bargain.

PETE. Okay.

RICH. I repeat, it was a bargain. You're going t'love it. It's in this bag. Saw it and thought of you.

PETE. So you said.

RICH. No, I said it were a bargain. Right, you want t'stay, catch up with technology, yeah?

PETE. Sure.

RICH. 'N' this. Well, this is state of the art. Very desirable.

PETE. Enough of the sales pitch, Rich.

RICH. Even got… well, I think the best colour.

PETE. Stop faffing about, will yer.

RICH. Is that what I'm doing?

PETE. Just show me what it is.

RICH. I'm faffing about then –

PETE. Rich.

RICH. Alright, alright, alright here you go.

RICH *takes a Bluetooth headset, in its case, out of a plastic bag.*

PETE. What is it?

RICH. A Bluetooth.

PETE. A what-tooth?

RICH. Blue. It's.

PETE. That's black.

RICH. No. It's. You put it. You want t'open it? I'll open it.

RICH *opens the package.*

You put it. Clip it behind your ear. Right, let me show you.

RICH *starts to put the headset on* PETE*'s ear.*

PETE. What yer doing?!

RICH. Got t'put it…

PETE. Leaning on…

RICH. Only takes…

PETE. Give over. Stop it.

RICH. There.

The headset is connected to PETE *'s ear.* RICH *stares at* PETE. PETE *allows him to continue.*

This right. Now this, yeah, this transmits a signal to yer mobile. Basically it means that you use this as an earpiece. Talk into it. Walk around. Without having to carry your phone. What you doing?

PETE. I'm not wearing that.

RICH. Why?

PETE. Because I'd look like a right twat.

He takes it off. Silence. PETE *puts it back on.*

RICH. Suits you.

PETE. Bet it does.

RICH. Proper twat.

Pause.

You're smiling.

PETE. Yes.

RICH. You look weird when you smile.

PETE. Do I?

RICH. Creepy.

PETE. Right.

RICH. Like some sorta animal. Jackal. Hyena. Or like if vultures smiled they'd look like that.

PETE. Thanks.

RICH. You'll have to practise. That's all I'm getting at. If it's going to become a regular thing.

Silence.

PETE. People actually use these?

RICH. Yes.

PETE. Fucking hell.

Pause.

Yer not tekin the piss?

RICH. No.

Pause.

PETE. Swear people walk round like this?

RICH. Yes.

PETE. Fuckin' hell.

Pause.

RICH. I'll be honest with yer I'm a fan of some advancements. Some, not all. This I think is okay. But I been thinking and it's been highlighted by my walk through town today. I been thinking this, Pete. I been thinkin' how much I hate the way people dress these days. Yer see old people and they always look smart. How they grew up. Men wear suits. Shirt and tie. They take pride. I want t'do that. I iron my chef's hat. Gets dirty in five minutes but I fucking do. What d'yer think's going t'happen when people my age get old? Going t'sit round in hooded tops. Hoodies 'n' ripped jeans. Haircuts like parakeets. There's going t'come a point in time when old people don't dress smart any more. That day is a sad day.

Silence.

PETE. Rich.

RICH. Yeah?

PETE. Would yer mind if I didn't live with you any more?

RICH. You don't want t'live with me?

PETE. Just asking.

No response.

Because I was thinkin' I might go away for a while. Move. Start again. Clean slate.

Pause.

Frank gave me some money.

Pause.

I want to become a plumber.

Pause.

You're my only connection with this place any more.

RICH. You gotta do what you reckon.

PETE. You wouldn't mind? Rich?

RICH. It's your life.

Silence.

Stupid little fucking bag.

PETE. Handbag.

RICH. Exactly.

Pause.

You were going to say goodbye, weren't you?

PETE. Course.

Silence.

RICH. Yer not dead, Pete.

PETE. Thanks, shorty.

RICH. Fuck off.

Silence.

Will you stay a minute, I'd like your help. Will you help me?

PETE *nods.*

Wait there.

RICH *returns moments later with some crowbars.*

These were under the sink.

PETE. Right.

RICH *gets on his knees and starts to rip the carpet up.* PETE
looks on, confused.

RICH. Come on.

PETE *watches for a couple more seconds then get on his knees and, after looking at* RICH, *joins in.*

Always hated this fuckin' carpet.

PETE *stops. Watches* RICH *for a second or two.*

PETE. No wonder those fuckin' shelves fell down. You have no idea about fuckin' DIY, do you? Look.

PETE, *slowly and methodically, starts to rip up the carpet.* RICH *watches.* RICH *starts to copy* PETE'*s method as the lights fade.*

The End.